MAKING FACES 3

by Susan Bonser

Making Faces 3
Food Art Inspired by Renaissance Artist Giuseppe Arcimboldo and Dall•E2 AI

ISBN: 9798393128173
Imprint: Independently published

The images in this book were generated using natural language digital AI tool DALL-E2 then retouched and prepped for publication using Adobe Photoshop and InDesign. Some of the text was written using ChatGPT, then edited in Microsoft Word. Any resemblance to previously published work is purely coincidental and unintentional.

You can email us at pennjournaloel@gmail.com.
See our other publications at http://thebonsers.com
All content © 2023 Susan Bonser

Introduction

The concept of art made from food is not a new one. The Germans imagined Schlaraffenland, a place where birds flew dressed and ready to eat, the rivers ran with milk—a precursor to the Hansel & Gretel folk tale. Even the Bible imagined a land of milk and honey. In fine art, Renaissance painter Giuseppe Arcimboldo is well known and widely imitated for assembling food to look like portraits. We chose to adopt this very old idea to experiment with making more contemporary photographic images, with crisp studio lighting and simple backgrounds using an AI graphic tool. Unlike Asian food art that is often intricately sculpted (and gorgeous) our goal was to make images representing faces by the proximity of the natural elements. They might be sliced or stacked but there are few places where you would have to sculpt to achieve the ideas shown here with real food.

AI is a wonderful tool to incorporate into many different creative processes. Artists might use it to imagine worlds or characters. They then might use those generative visual results in combination or create new art in other mediums such as digital imaging, sculpture, paint or collage. We used AI here to fulfill our imagined 3-dimensional food art—designs for faces, animals, birds, and reptiles created entirely from beautiful fruits, vegetables, herbs and flowers.

We share here just a few of the more than 200 food art images that we generated using AI. These images can be a source of inspiration for creating your own AI images, for creating food art using real produce, or for moving the idea to another medium. Of course, you can simply enjoy the creativity and beauty of the images. They might even make you smile.

These images were created using natural language prompts, revised to achieve the results we imagined, using the OpenAI Dall•E2 public version of the software. We then took the images into Adobe Photoshop to retouch anomalies and to prep them for publication using Adobe InDesign. Text was written in Microsoft Word. Some of the content was generated in OpenAI ChatGPT then edited.

Simple Faces

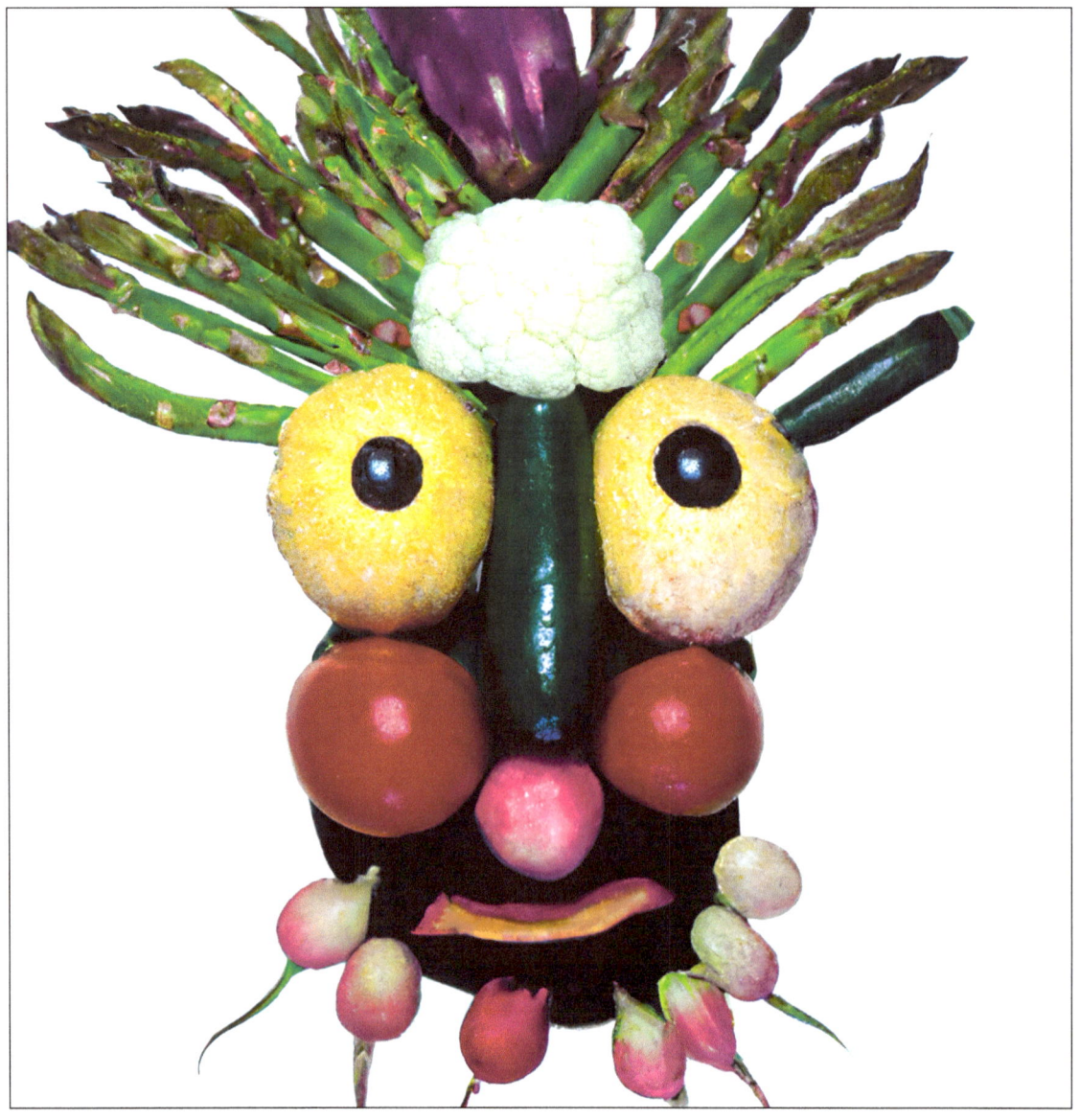

Right, Food can look like a face simply by the proximity of the pieces. Half of an acorn squash, a tomato, a piece of melon, a couple of slices of cucumber, a red grape cut in half and two raisins for eyes. A sunflower on the top for some crazy hair or a hat. *Left*, You can imagine the vegetables that might be used to make this face. Black olives and mushroom caps for eyes, asparagus for hair, a Kirby cucumber nose, tomato cheeks. Hold it all in place with something like hummus or cream cheese. (We wouldn't use toothpicks—don't want someone to get an ouch.)

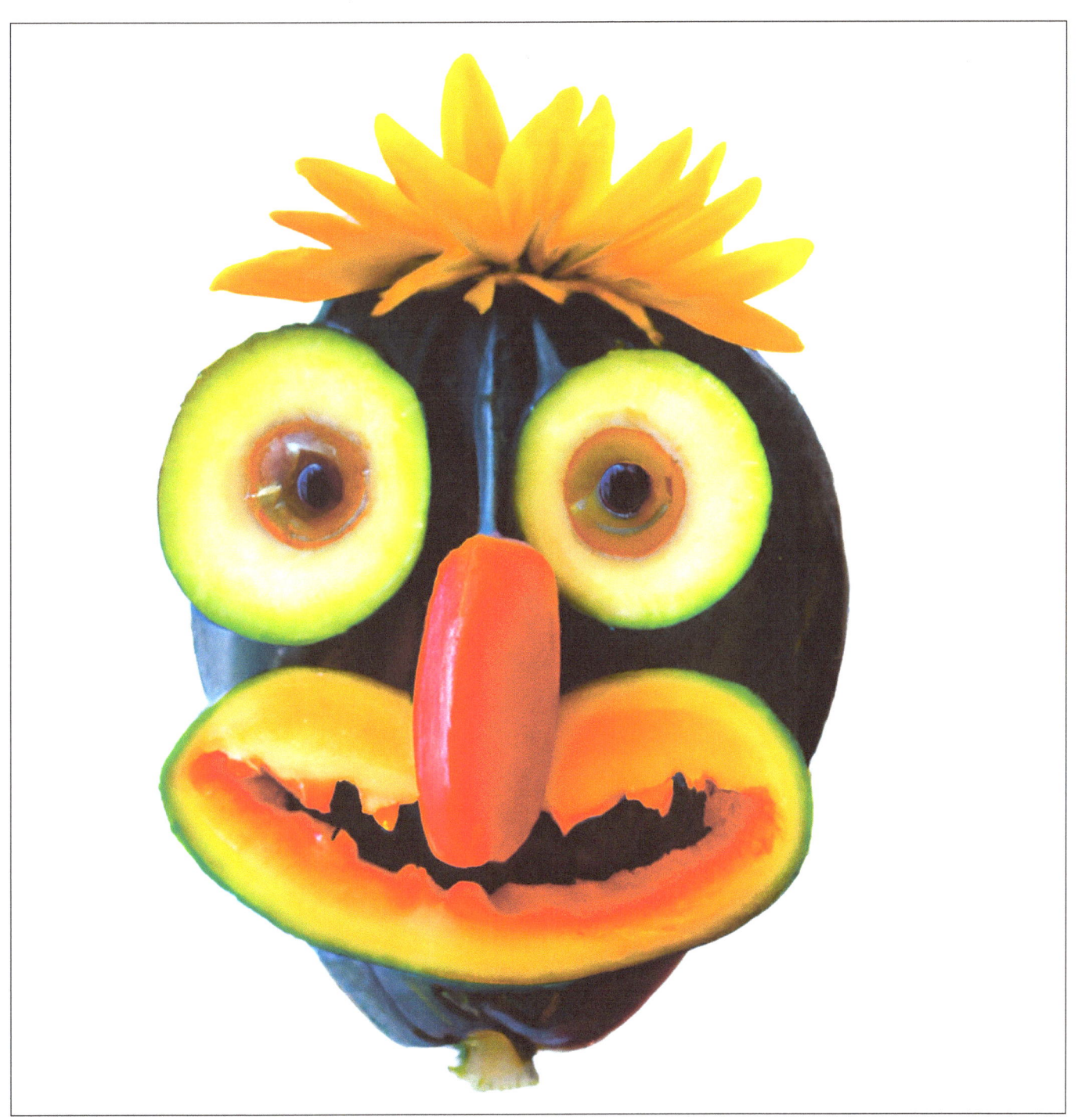

Simple Faces

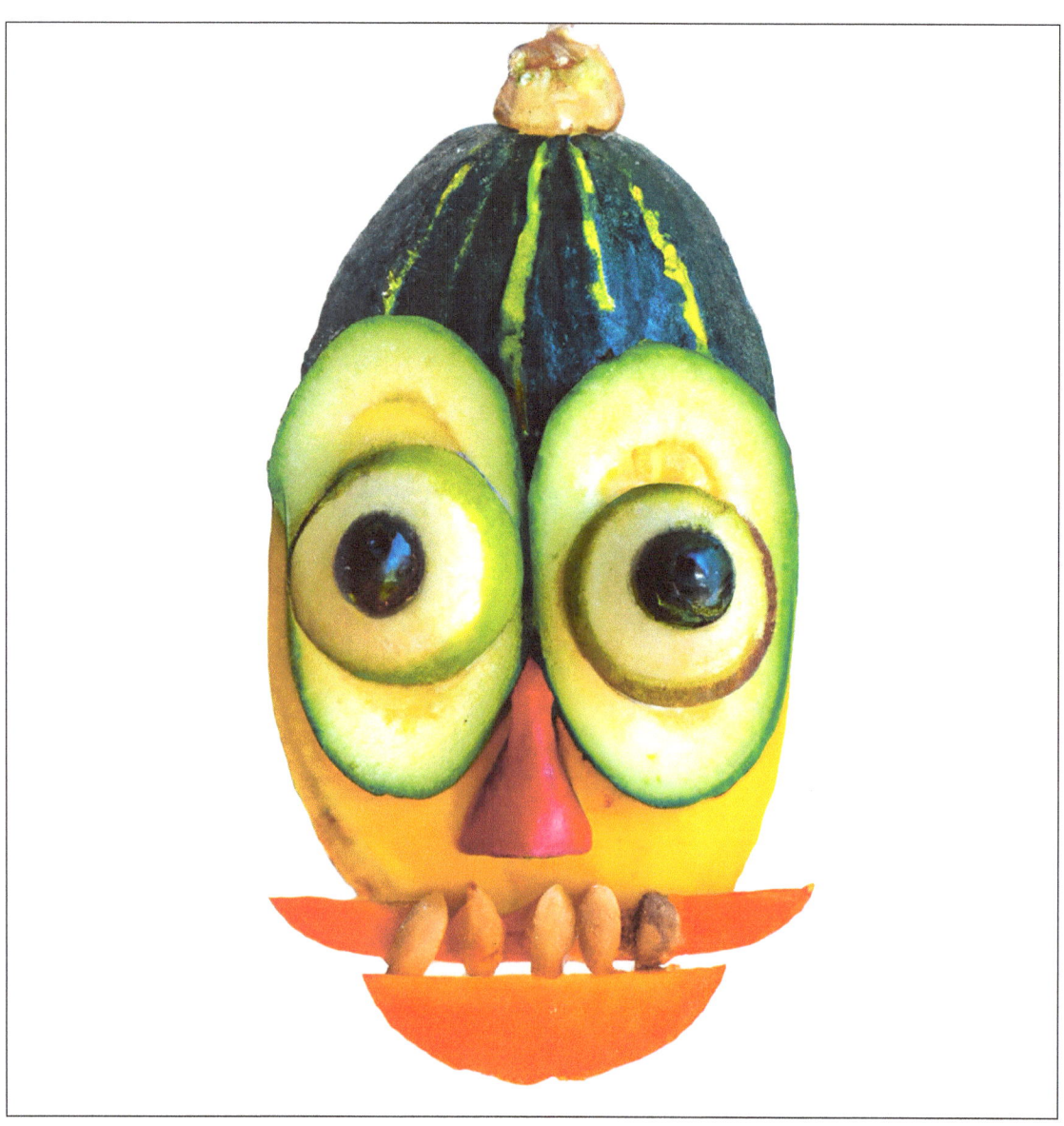

Right, The simplest arrangement of vegetables can suggest a face. Lettuce, cherry tomatoes and a carrot. If you grow your own you have the advantage of finding oddball shapes that might suggest a mouth. *Left*, Another simple face is made by stacking slices. It could start with a melon then adding slices of cucumber, pickles and black olives for eyes. The smile might be slices of mango or orange pepper, with almonds for teeth. The image is meant to inspire you to use the produce you love and what is available at the time of your food art creation.

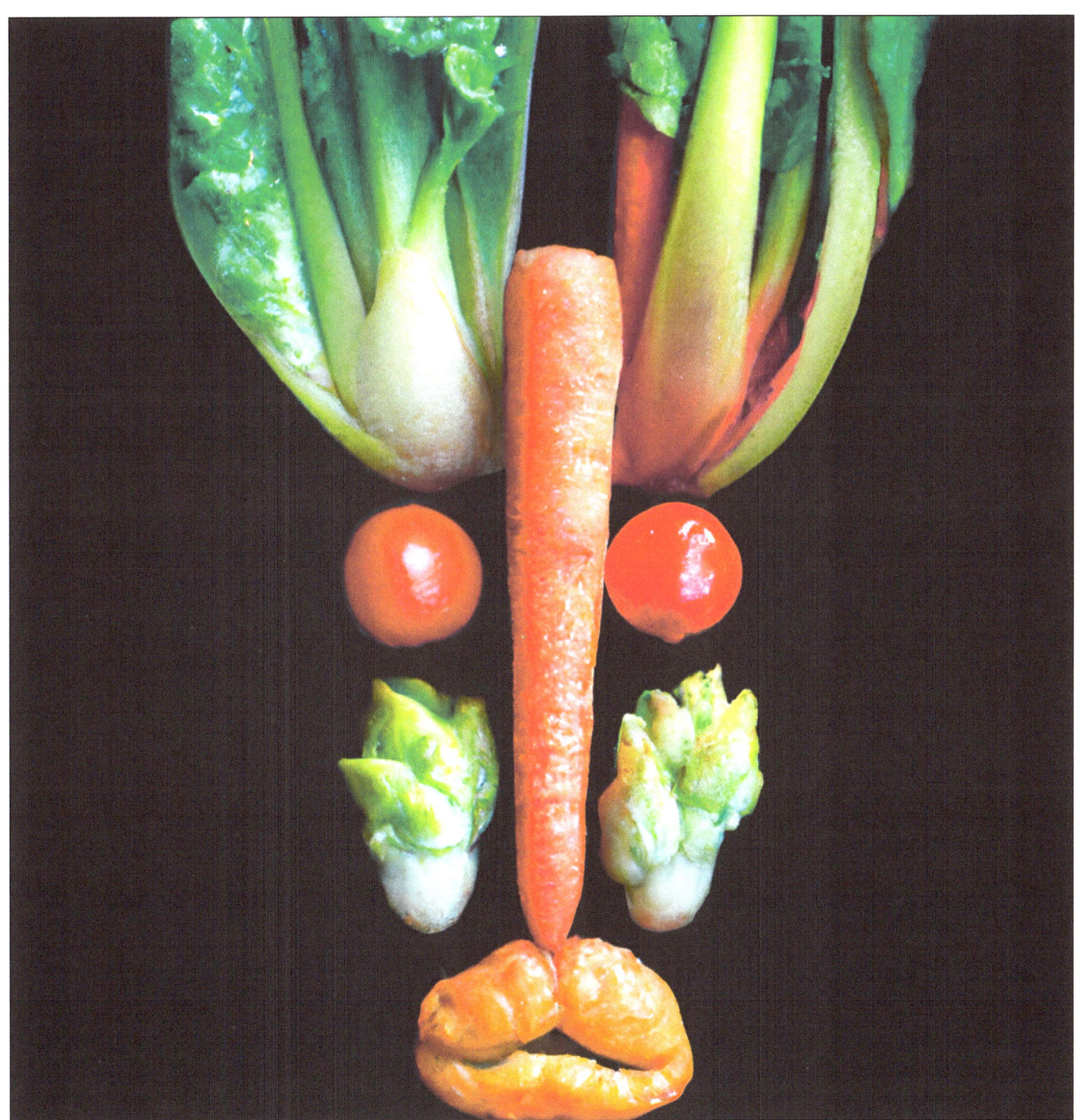

More Complex Faces

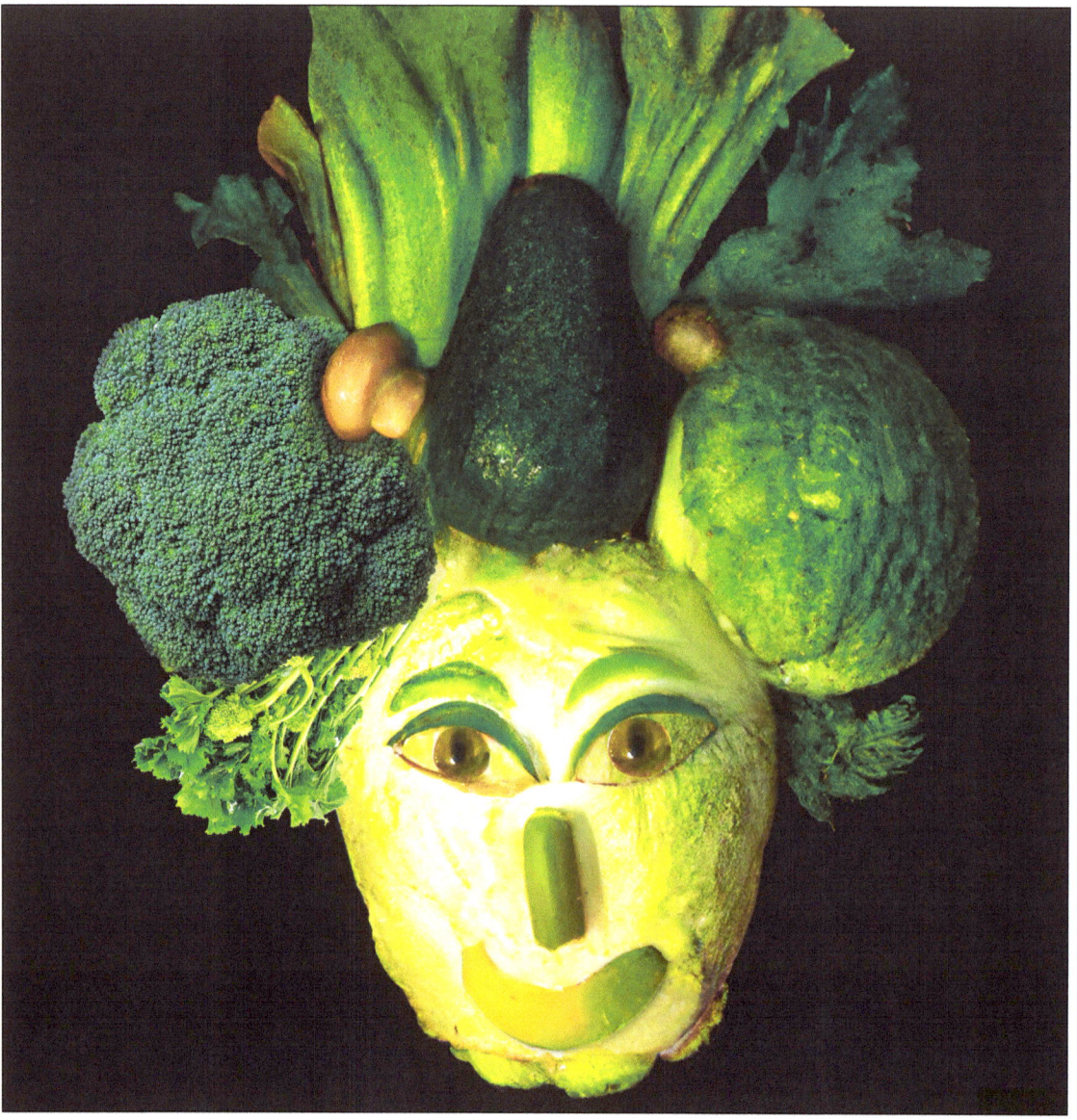

Right, This face reminded us of Kabuki Theater. It started with a white head shape that might be lettuce or a melon. It could even be cheese. Stacked on are fresh peas, slices of what could be red pepper for lips and pear for cheeks. The eyes are represented by a red-flesh fruit or vegetable surrounded by herb leaves for eyelashes. A peppercorn could finish the eyes. Surrounding the head we find peas in the pods, potatoes, a lemon and a head of lettuce.

Left, This face uses a monochromatic scheme in choosing the variety of fruits and vegetables used to bring it to life. It starts with a head of lettuce. We see broccoli, broccoli raab, avocado, mushrooms, leeks, celery for a nose, and an arc of lime peel for a mouth.

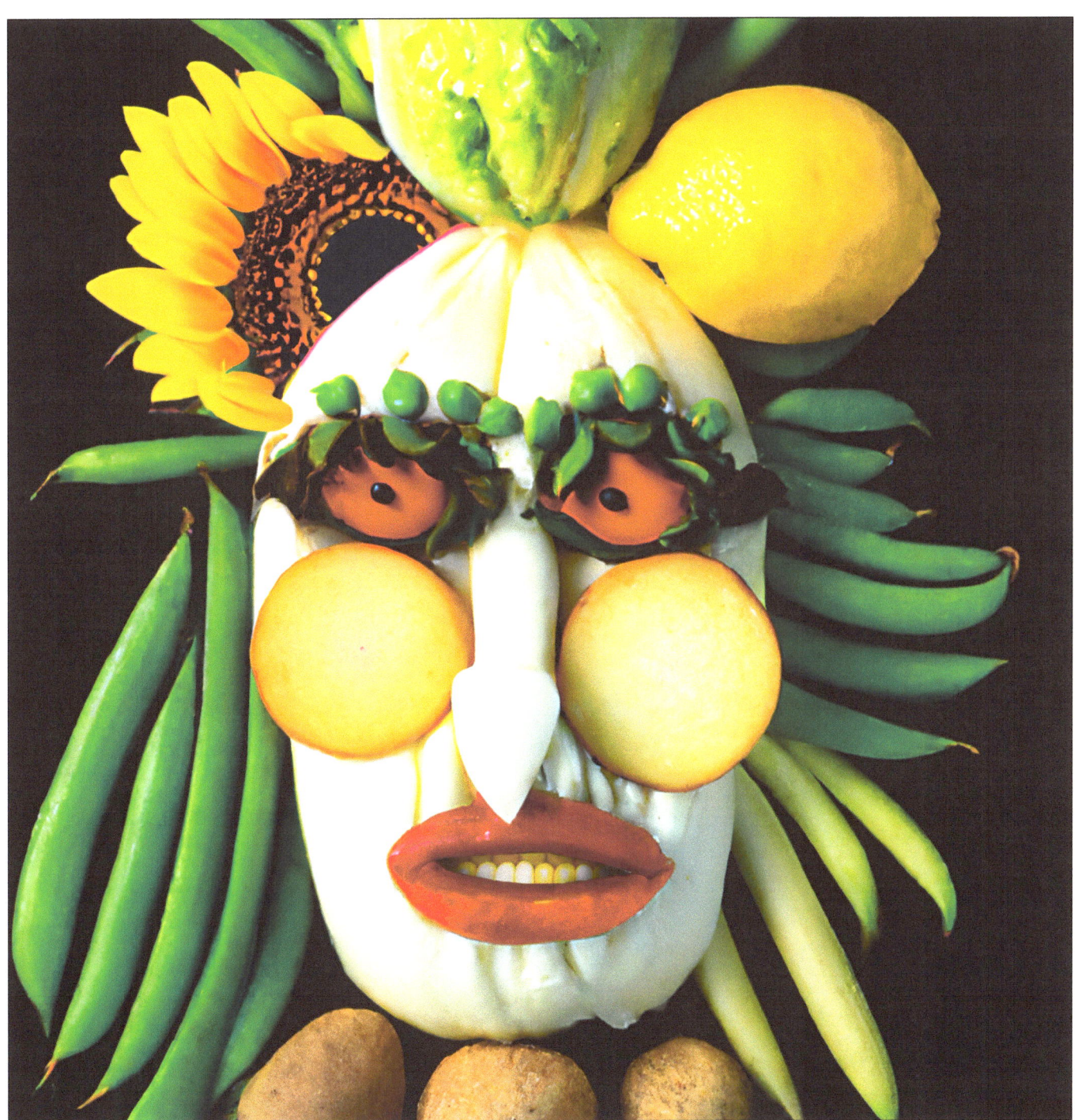

MAKING FACES 3

More Complex Faces

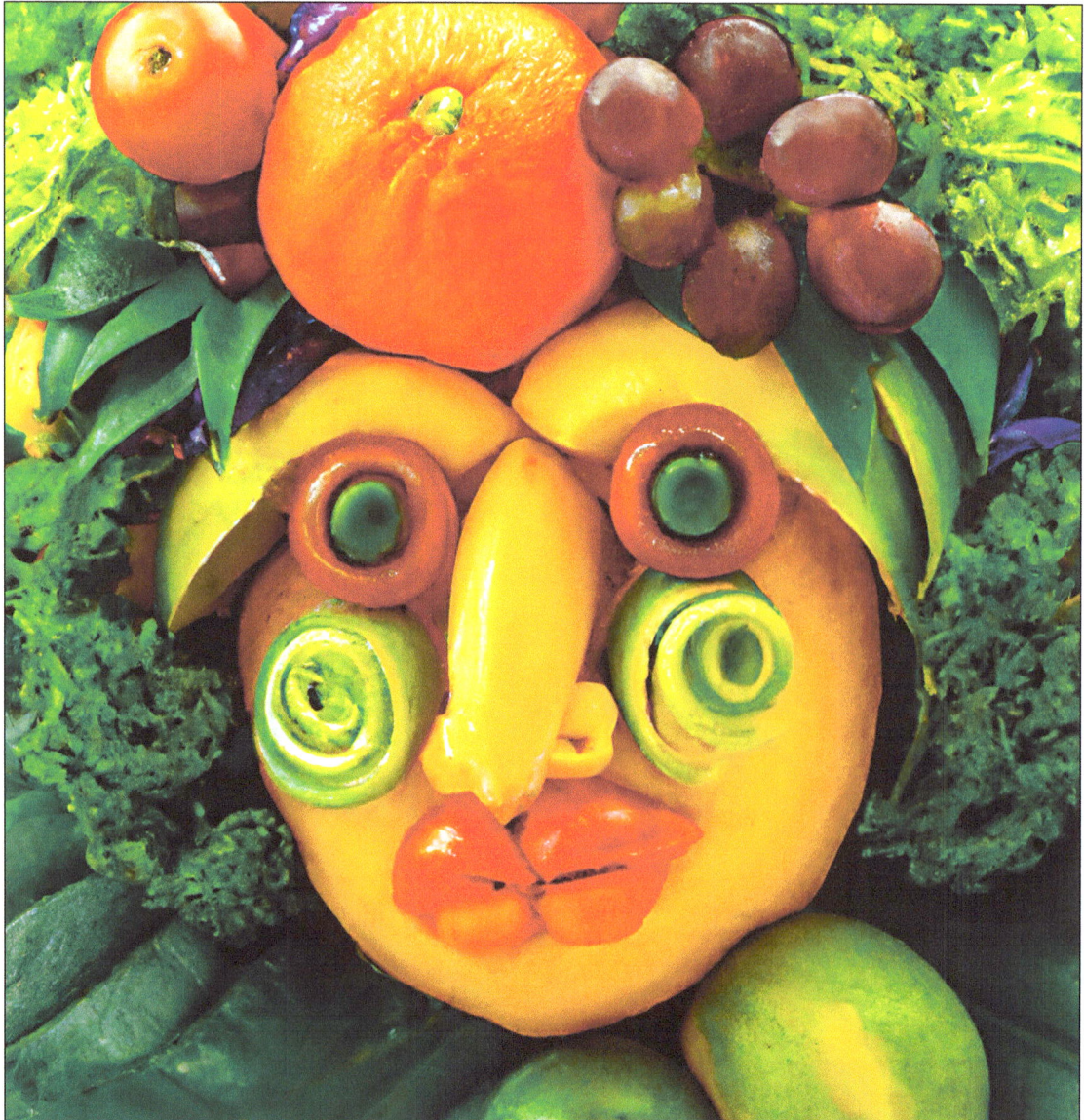

Right, One of our favorite parts of this face is the cherry tomato eyes wrapped in what looks to us to be red onion sections. We love the berries in the nose. The lips might be shaped by a slice in the base then painted red with food color. *Left*, Both faces on these pages look like they could start with a base of mango or melon. The lips here look like pieces of red pepper. The nose might be a sweet banana pepper. The cheek twirls could be celery, cucumber or squash sliced very thin. There are a lot of different fruits and vegetables that could be used to achieve this look.

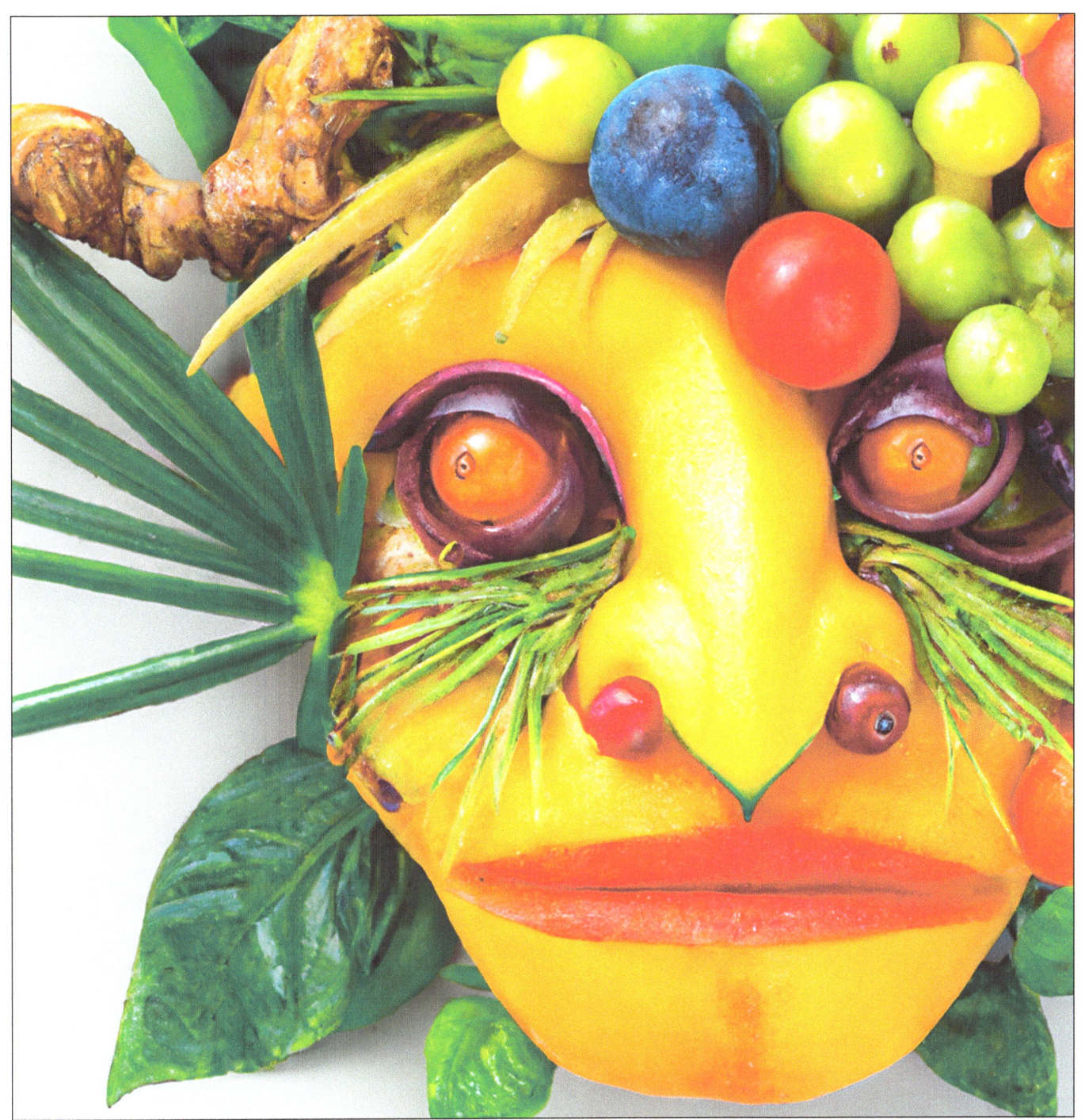

More Complex Faces

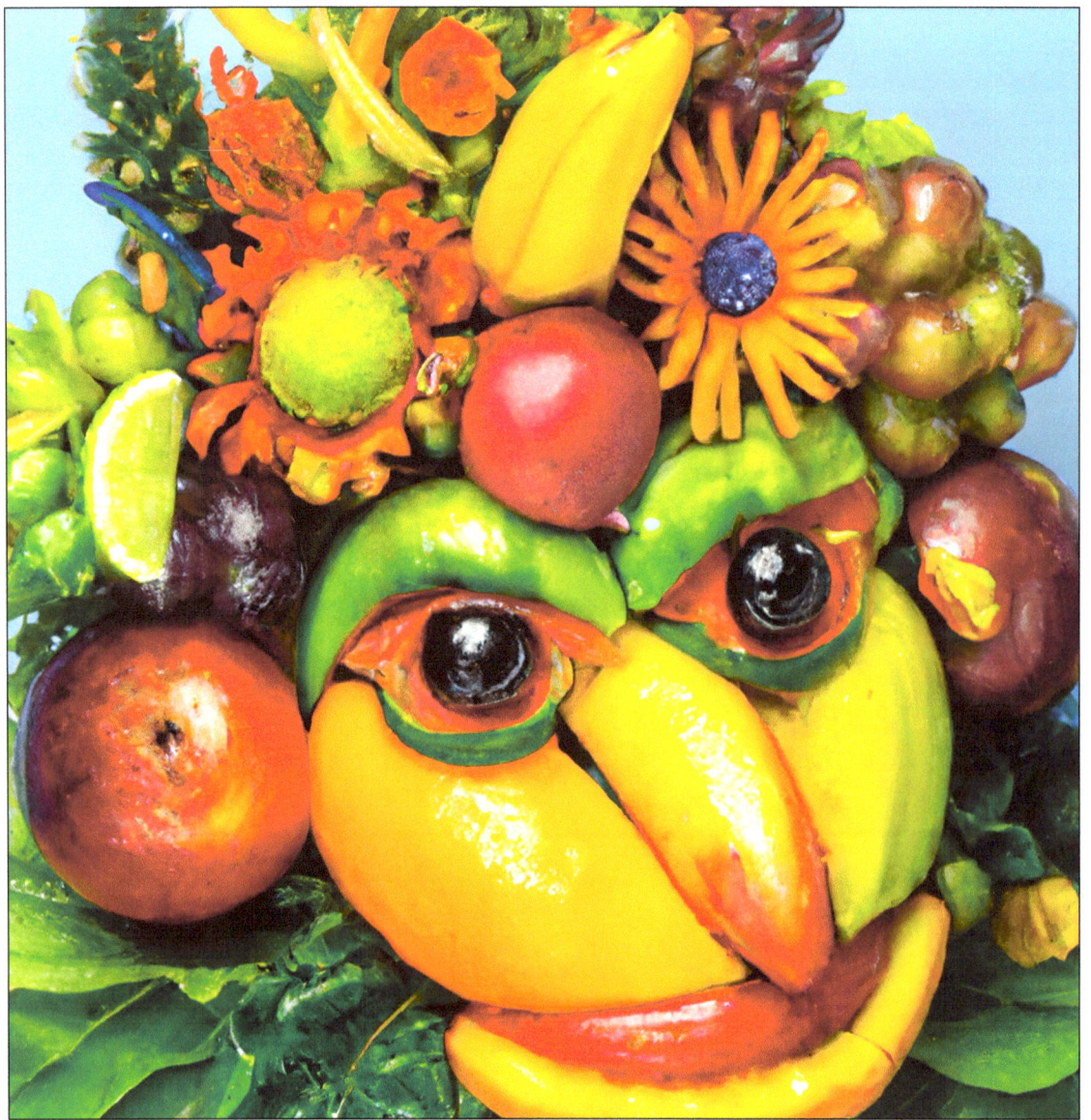

Right, This face might include Lychee or Rambutan. The eyelashes could be Rambutan shells with melon or a wedge of lemon and a blueberry defining each eye. The green stalk coming out of the headdress could be stem lettuce, but you could use any long green vegetable in its place. The eyebrows might be Cecropia Fruit, also called gummy worm fruit. *Left*, The fruits used in this face could be any of the tropical fruits like mango or melon, a finger banana for the nose and in the headdress, half moons and slices of lime rind could shape the eyelids with big purple grapes for the eyes.

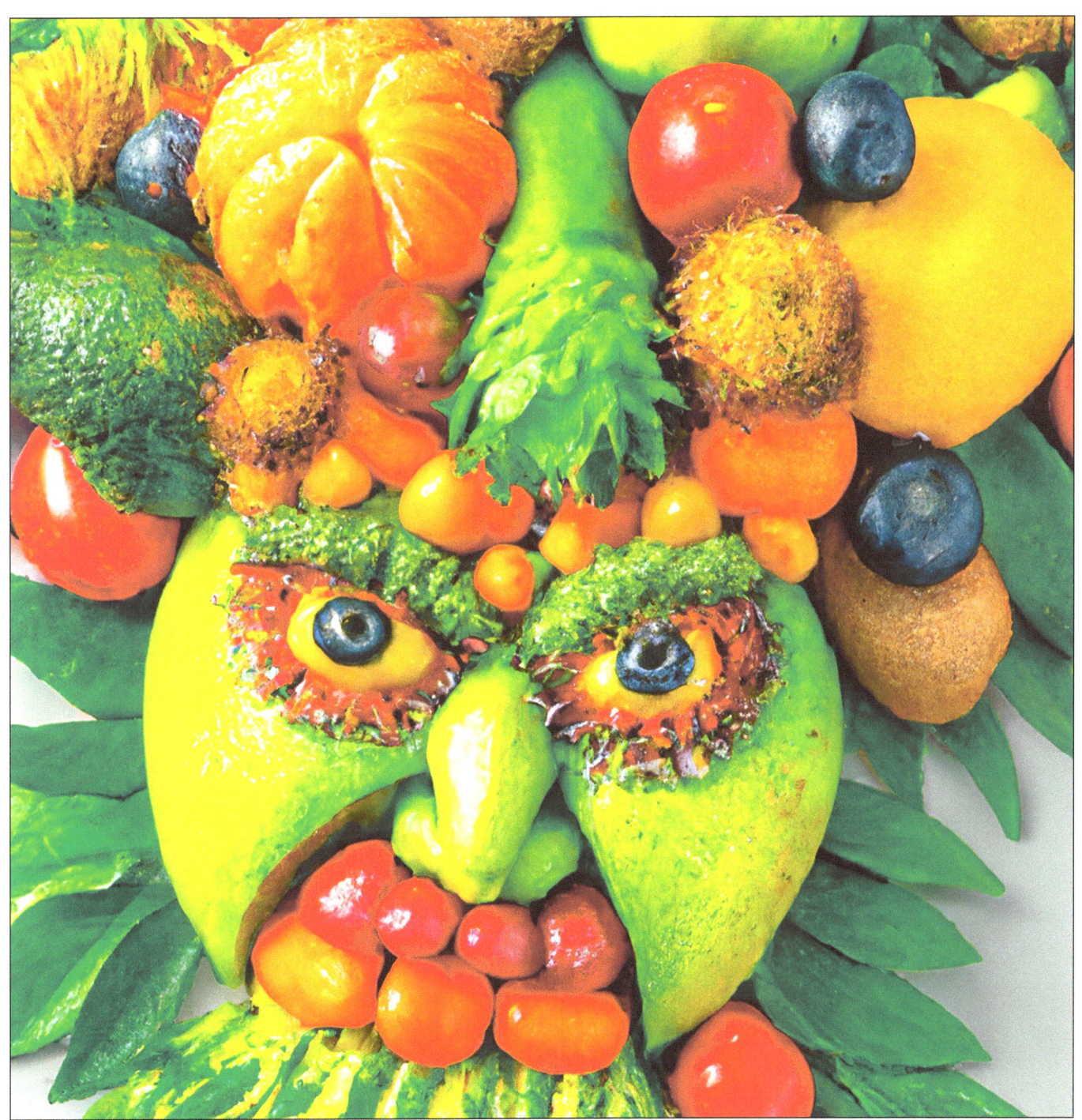

MAKING FACES 3

More Complex Faces

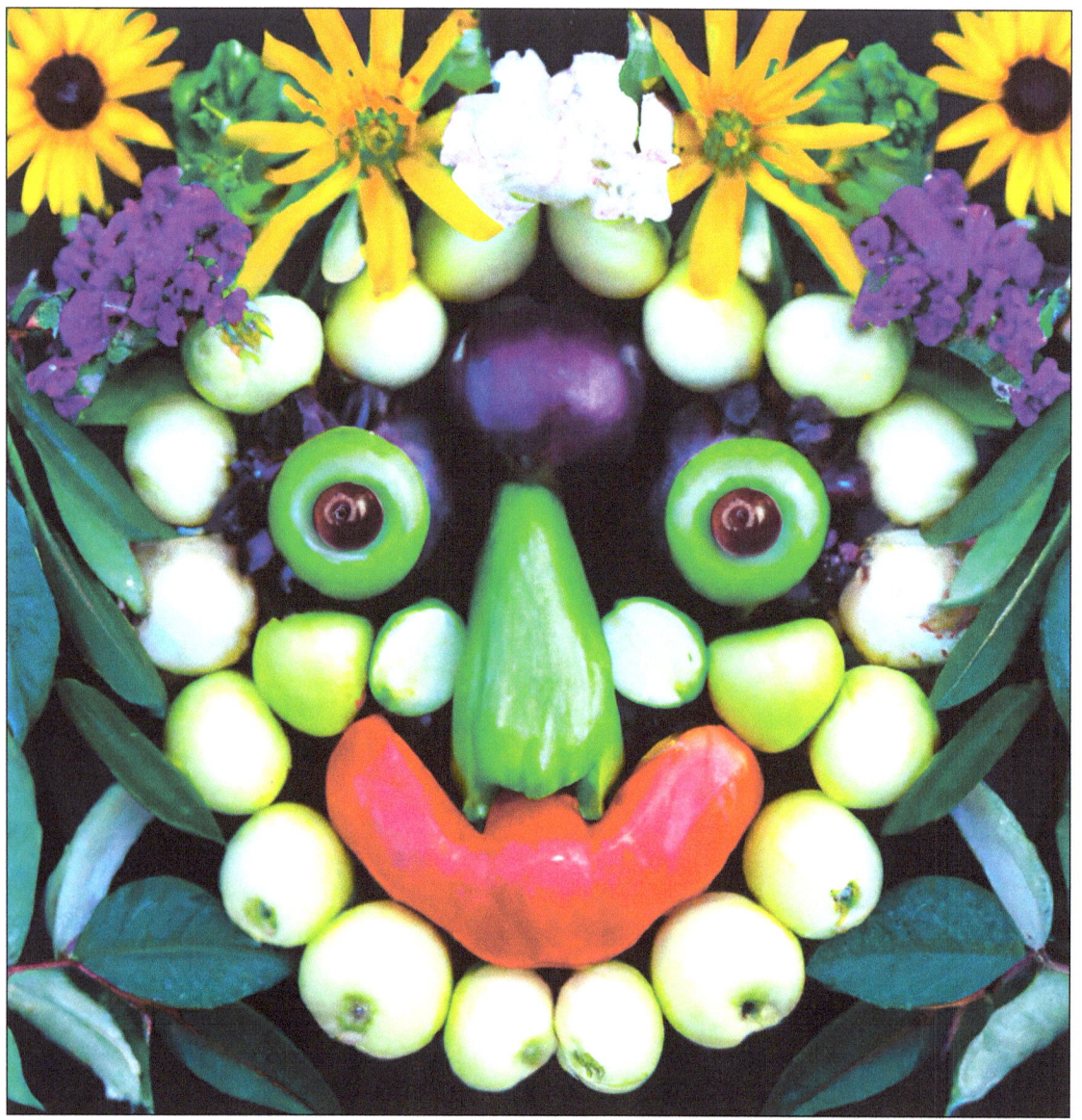

Right, The first thing we noticed about this face was the use of kumquats and yellow peppers. While the area around the mouth could be large corn kernels, they could also be pineapple niblets. The fruit at the top of the head could be peaches, persimmons, or any yellow-flesh fruit. Slices of pear or apple could define the eyes.
Left, This face is very straightforward. Lots of little apples or white onions define the face. Green apples for the eyes. The nose might be a pepper cut to shape. The mouth a section of red chile pepper or long red radish.

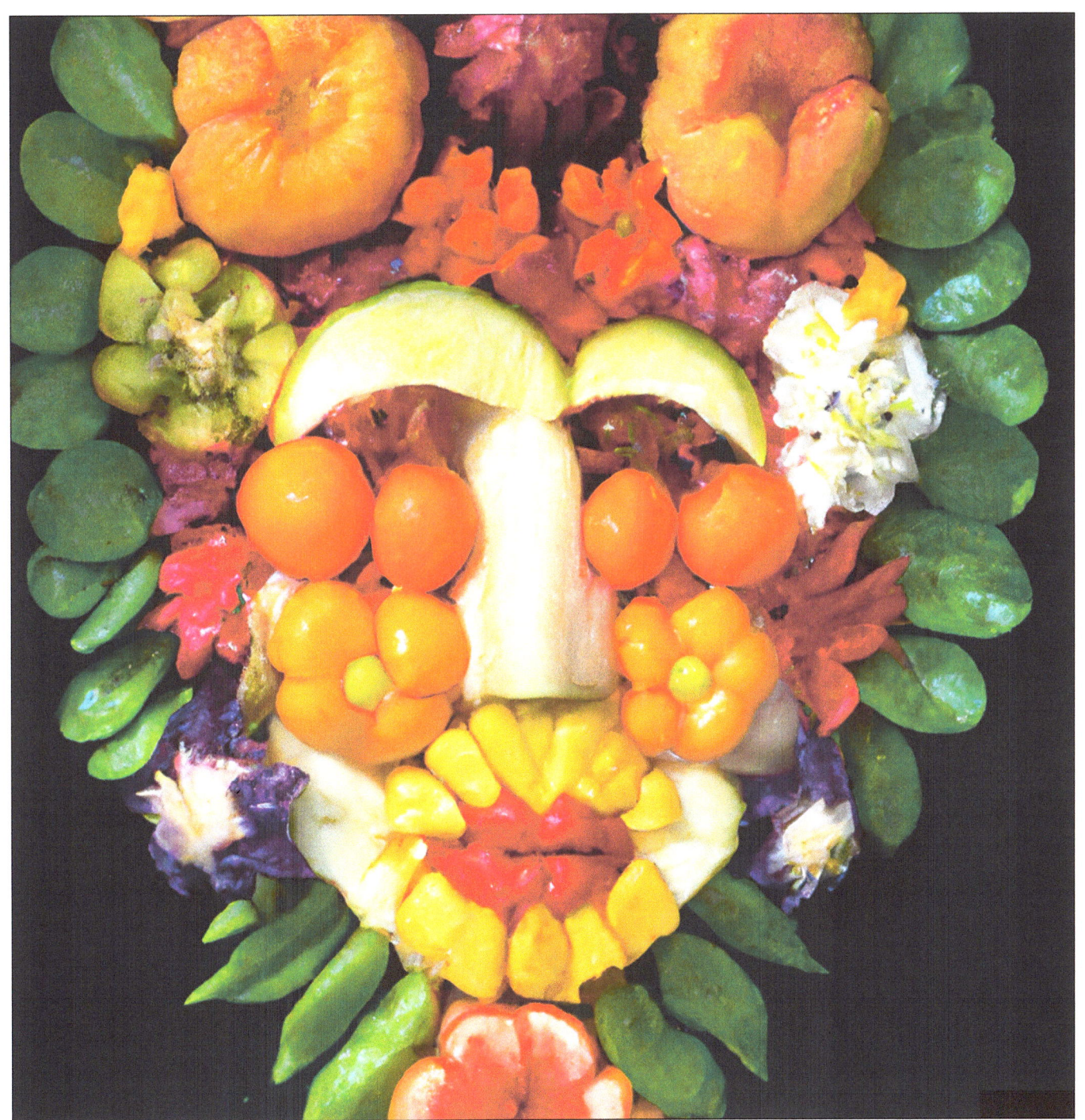

Animal Faces

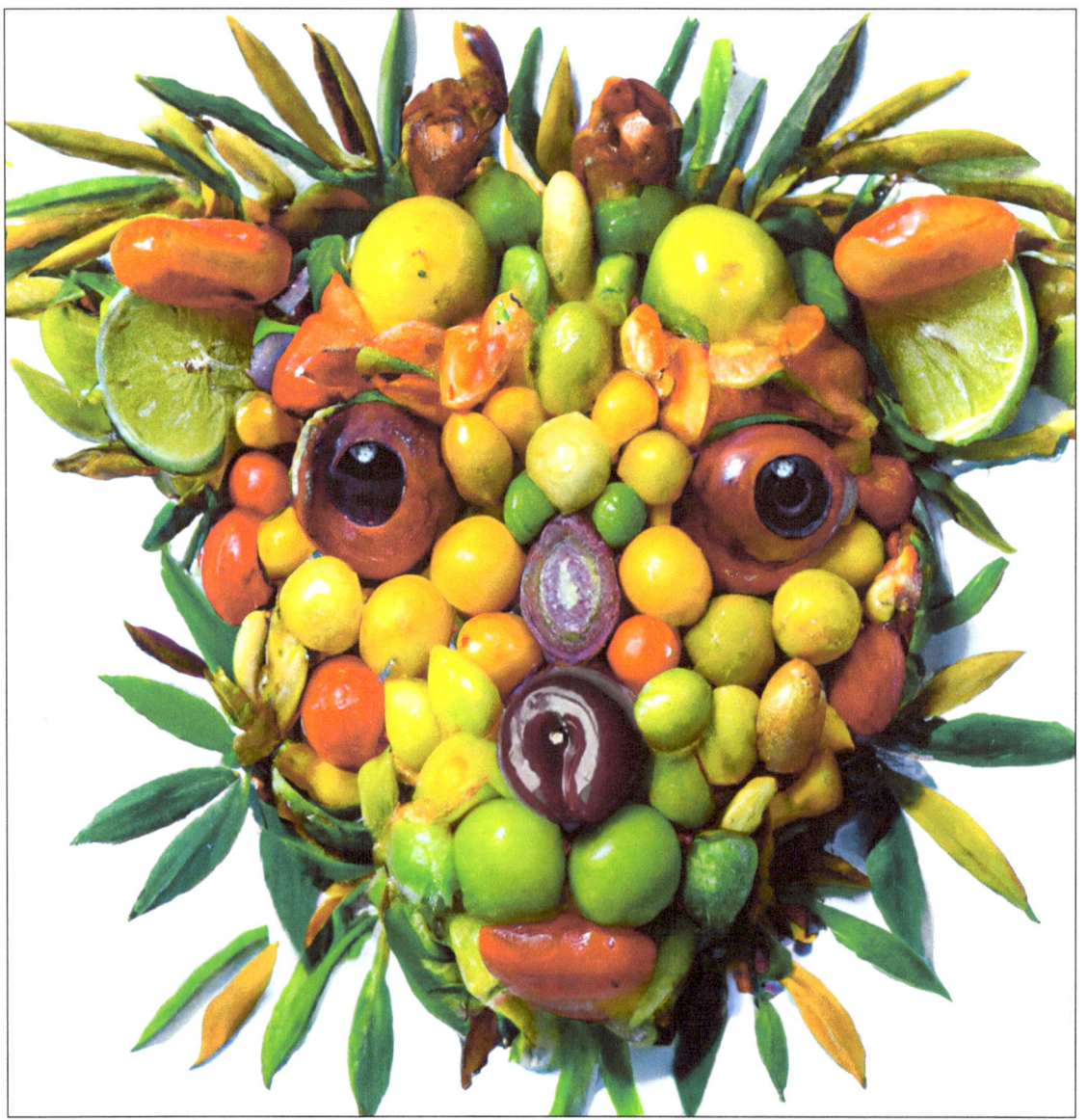

Right, This little dog uses very simple elements to shape his face. They could be small limes, cherry tomatoes, radishes and big purple grapes or black olives for eyes. The nose of both animals here could be a black sweet cherry, black plum, Concord grape or purple chile. *Left*, This little lamb has lime slices for ears. The face is shaped in much the same manner as the little dog with lots of small round fruits. The eyes are inset with a slice of black olive. The lip could be a slice of red pepper.

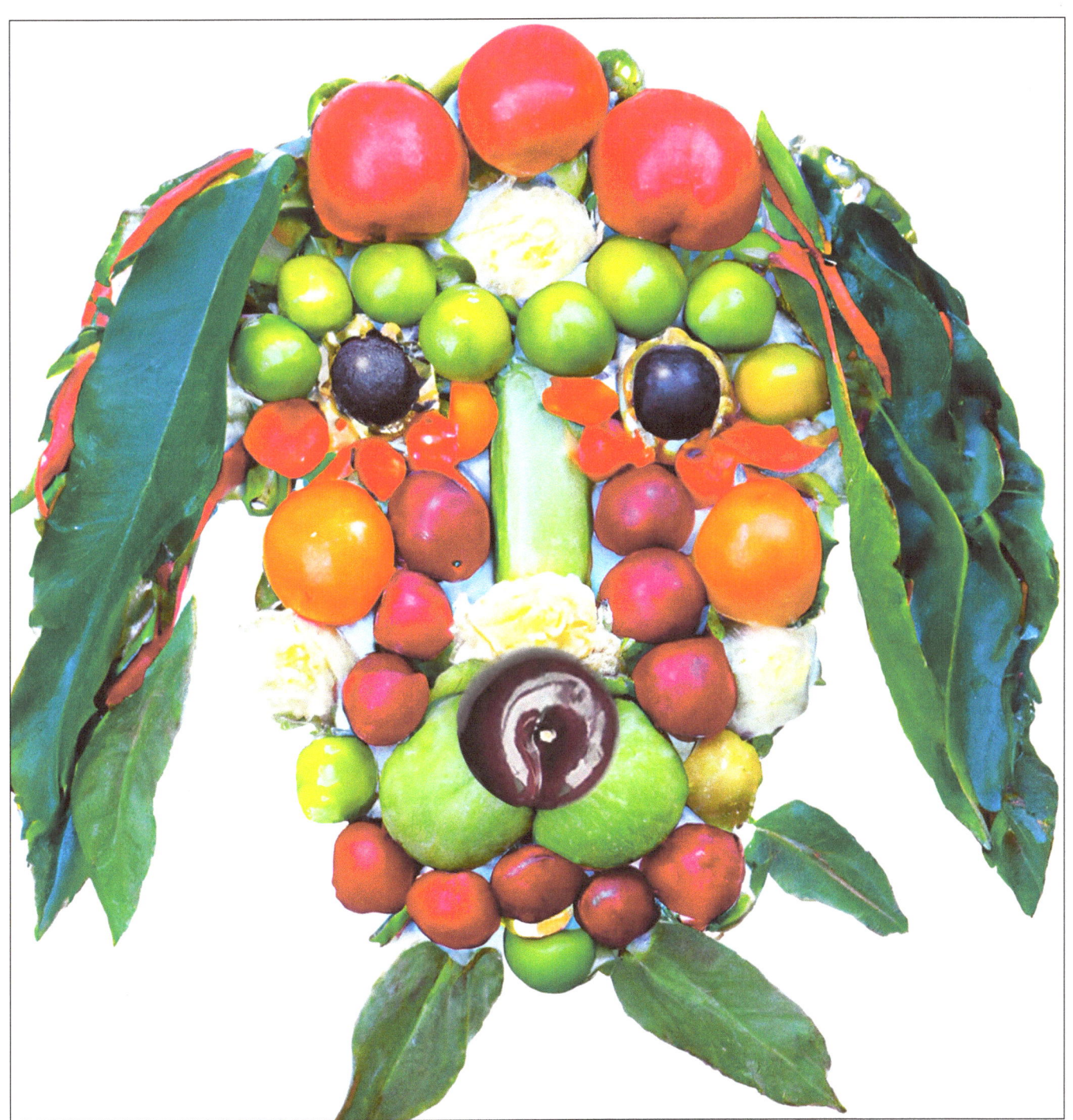

Animal Faces

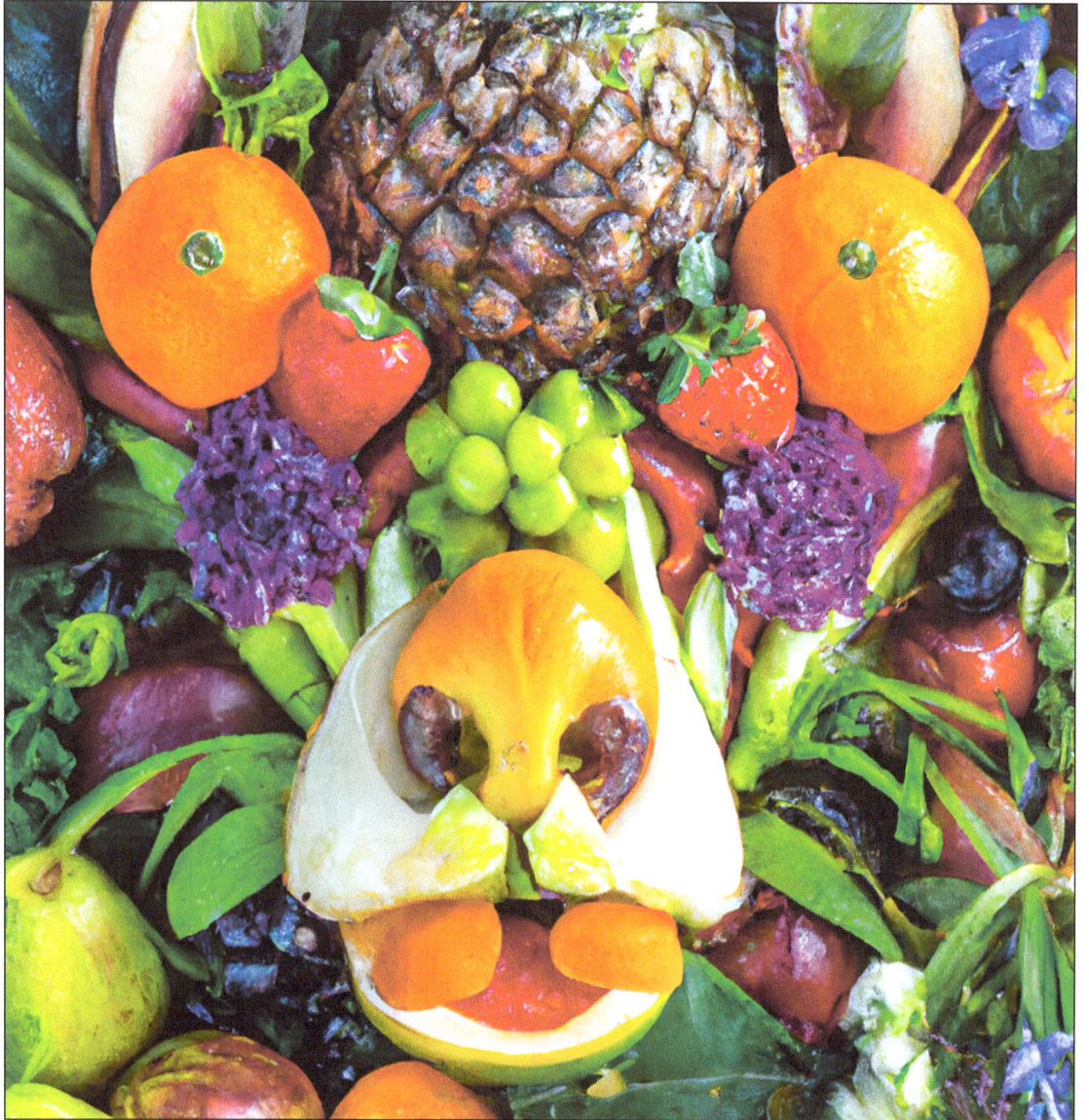

Right, Appropriately, this little rabbit is made up of mostly lettuce. She has clementines for feet and small fruits define her face. Strawberries, cherries, grapes and pieces of melon could be used. Her eyes look like a couple of shiny dried prunes but blackberries might work just as well.
Left, The goat uses common fruits such as oranges, strawberries, grapes and pears. Her nose looks like a persimmon with holes cut in and a red grape in each nostril. The top of her head might be a small pineapple or other tropical fruit of a similar texture. Lots of flowers and greens fill out her head. We would use a fig for each ear.

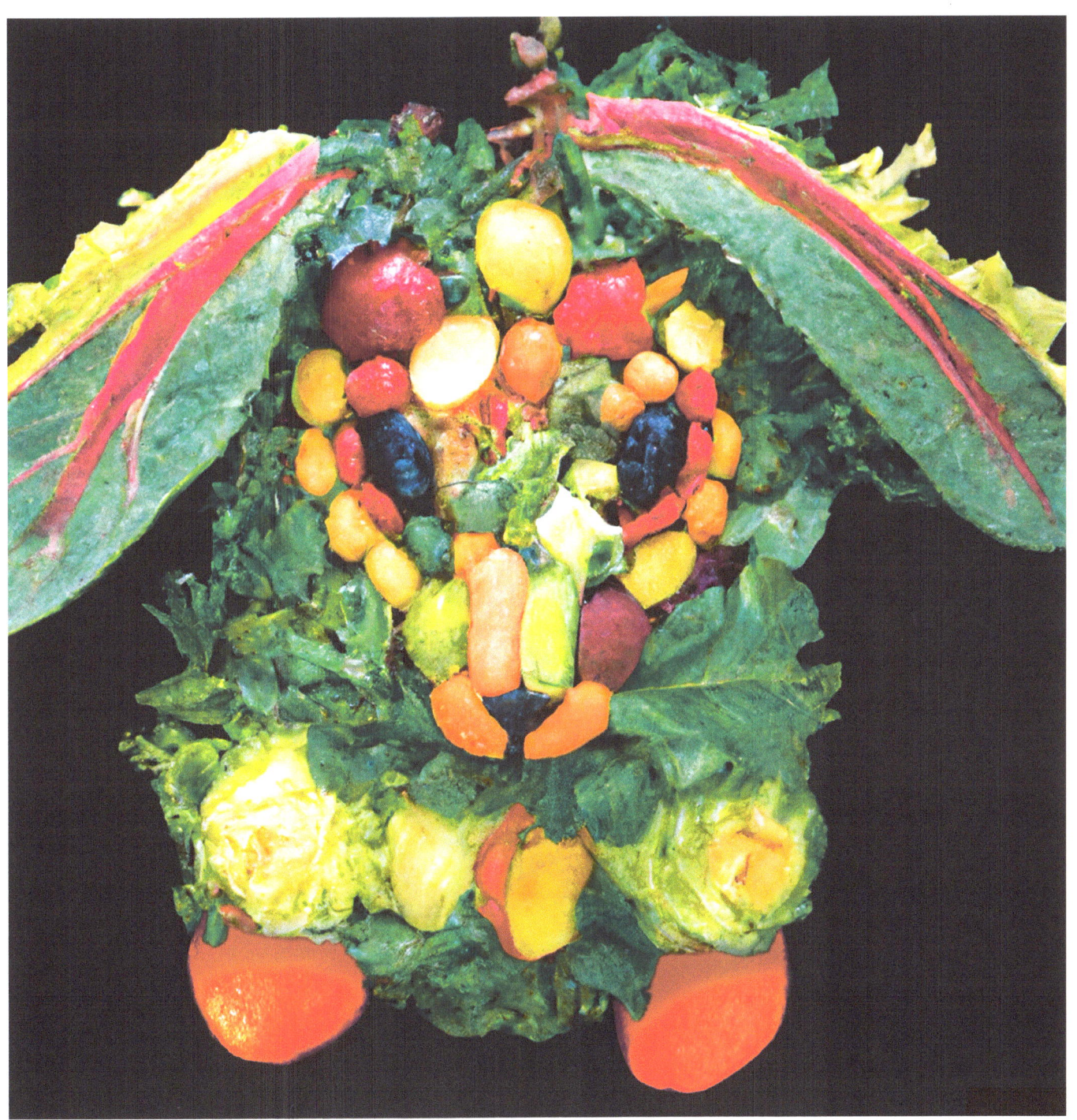

Fish & Reptile Faces

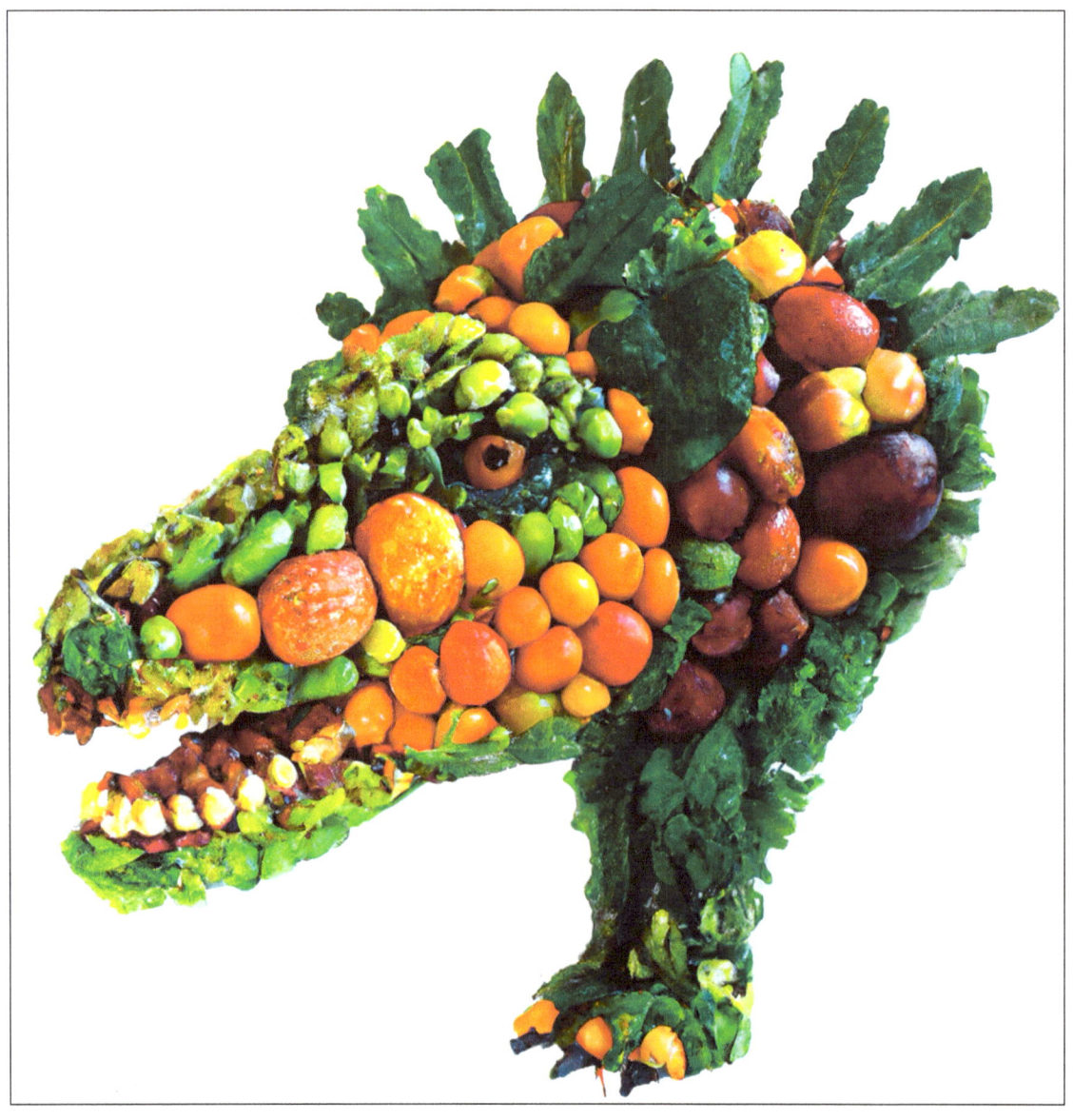

Right, The fish is covered with shiny round fruit like grapes and cherries. His mouth looks like slices of avocado. His nose a strawberry. His spiky tines could be aloe or agave, or any edible similarly-shaped leaf. His eye might be layered with slices of potato, pepper, and black olive.
Left, This dinosaur is also filled with small, shiny fruits just like the fish. He has spikes that could be many varieties of lettuce, arugula or even dandelion.

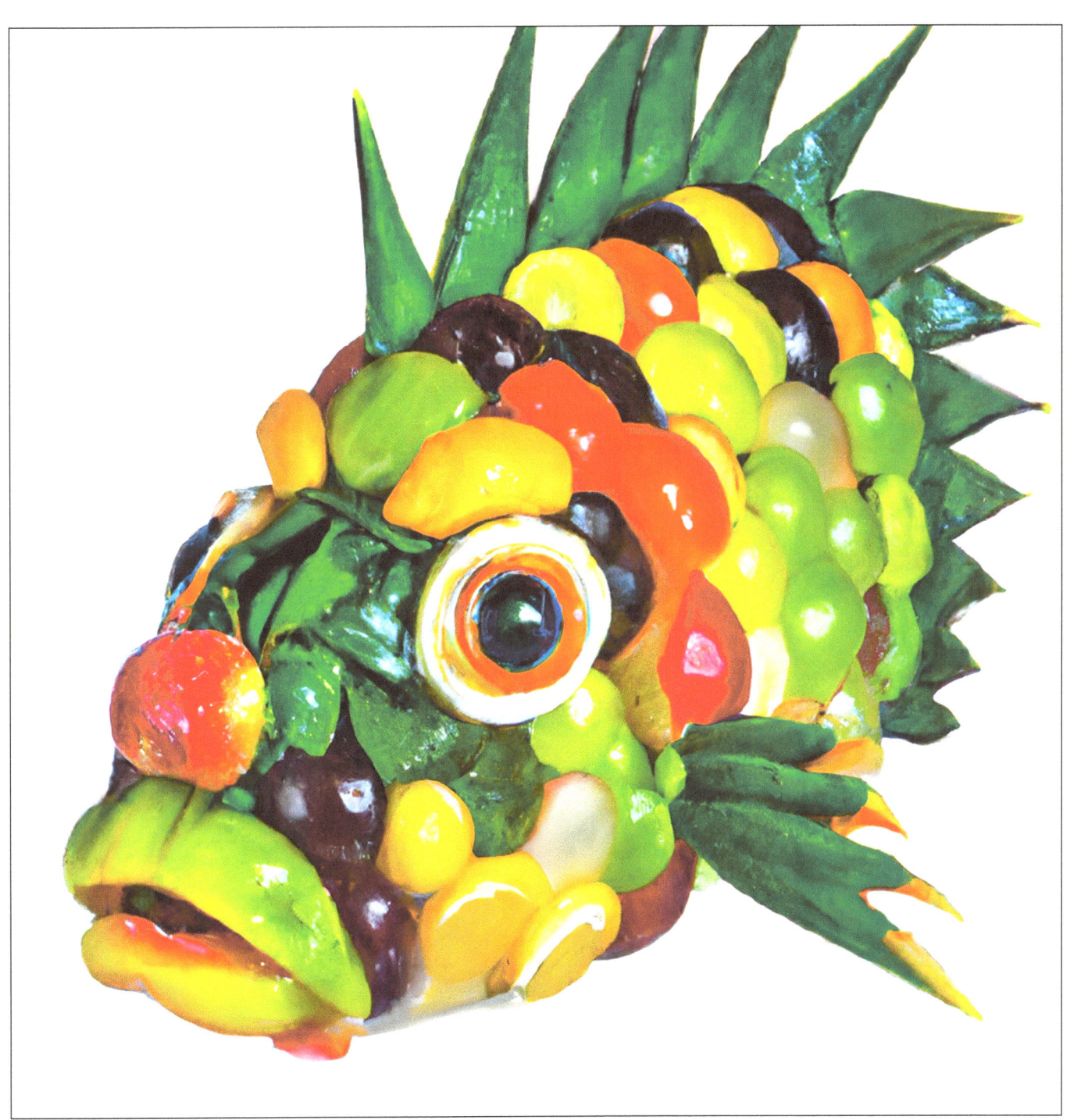

Fish & Reptile Faces

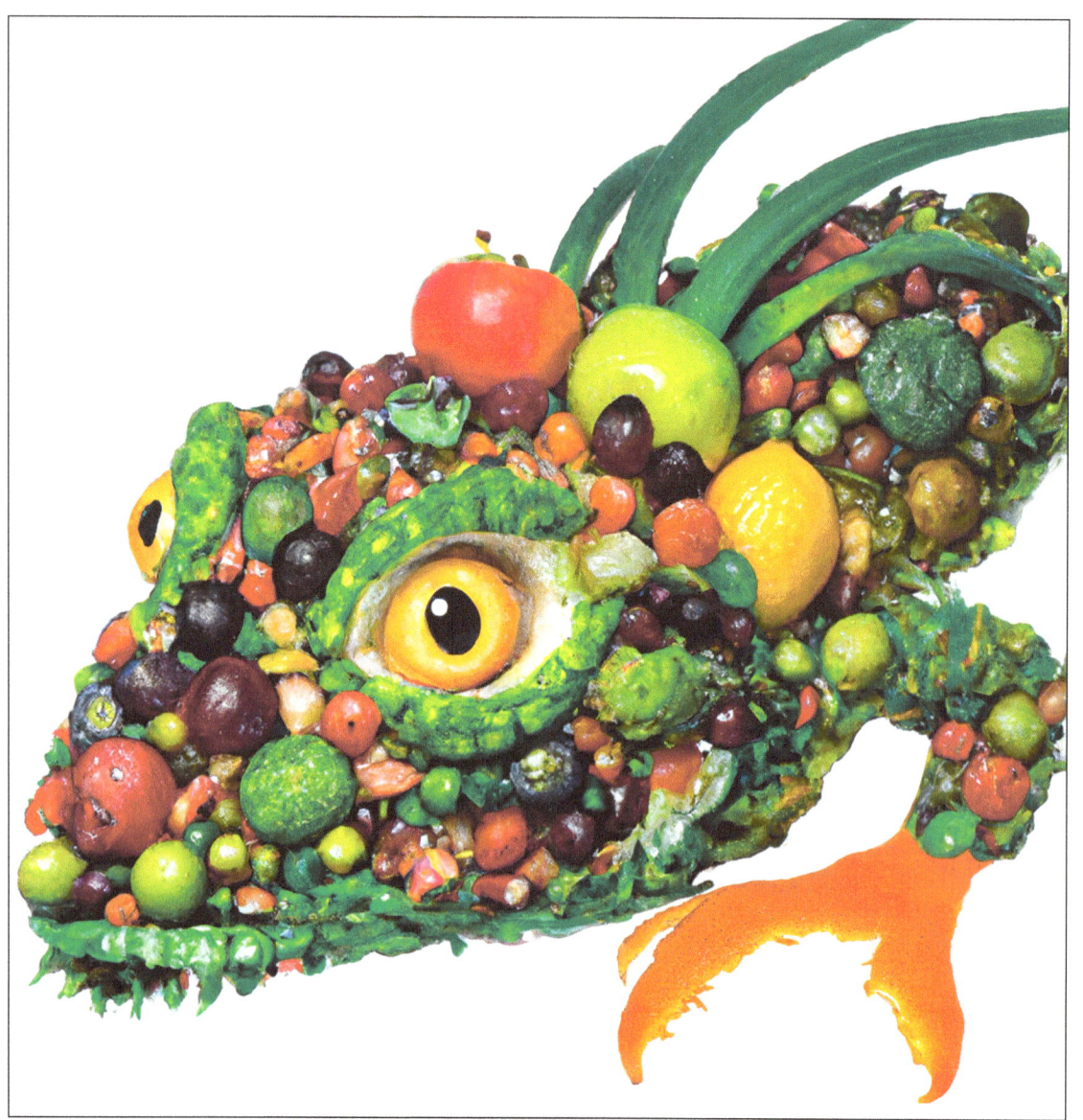

These Pages, Both of these creatures are filled with small shiny fruits and vegetables in a way similar to the dinosaur. Grapes, cherries, olives—there is an endless variety of foods that might be used. The first step in all of these animals is to decide what the base will be. We would use a loaf of bread or a block of cheese, then shape it a bit to the form of the animal. Again, we would stick the elements onto the base with hummus or a soft spreadable cheese. The iguana's spiky tines could be aloe or agave, or any non-toxic similarly-shaped leaf. His claws are cut out of a fresh clementine or orange peel.

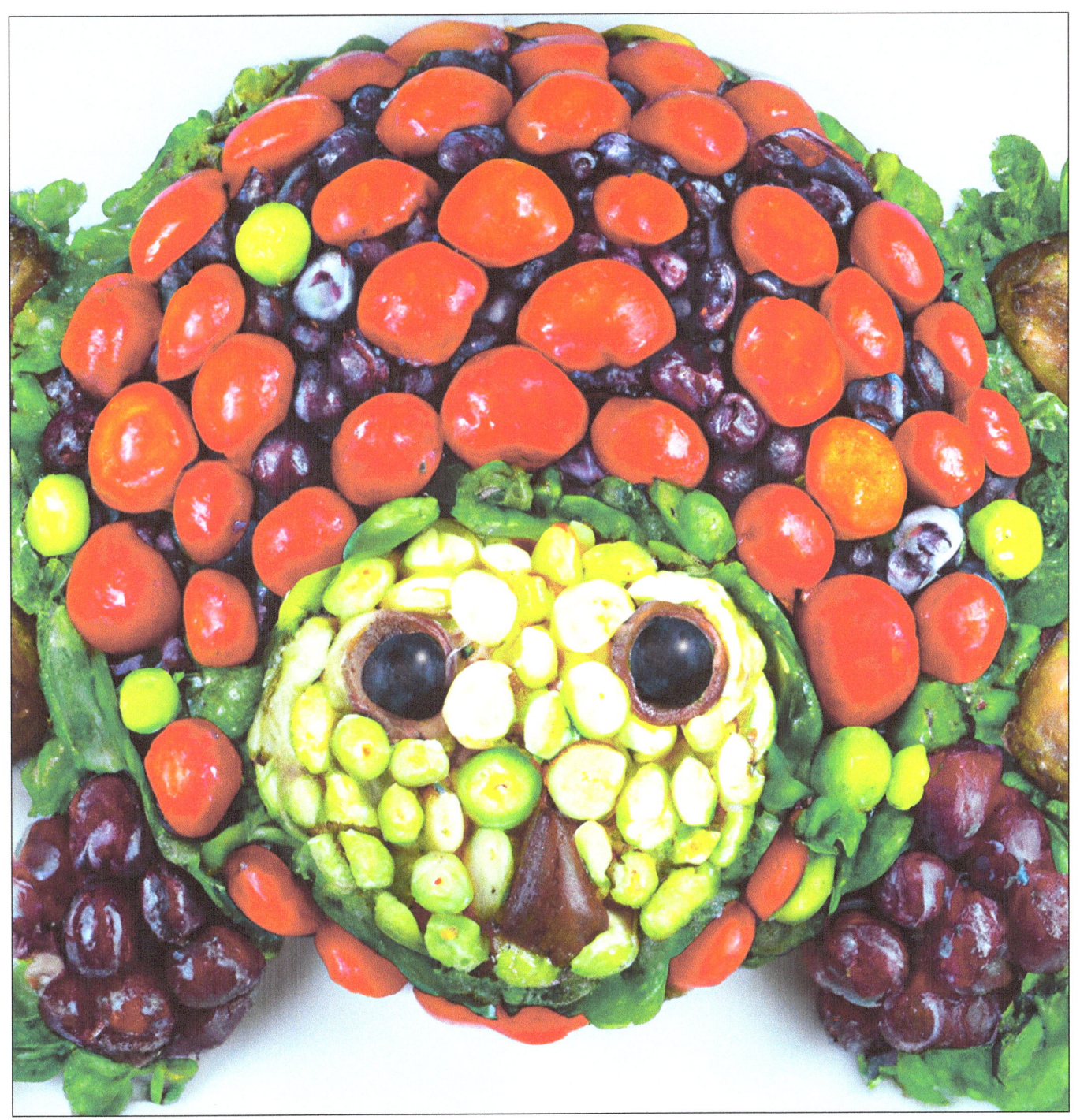

MAKING FACES 3   23

Fish & Reptile Faces

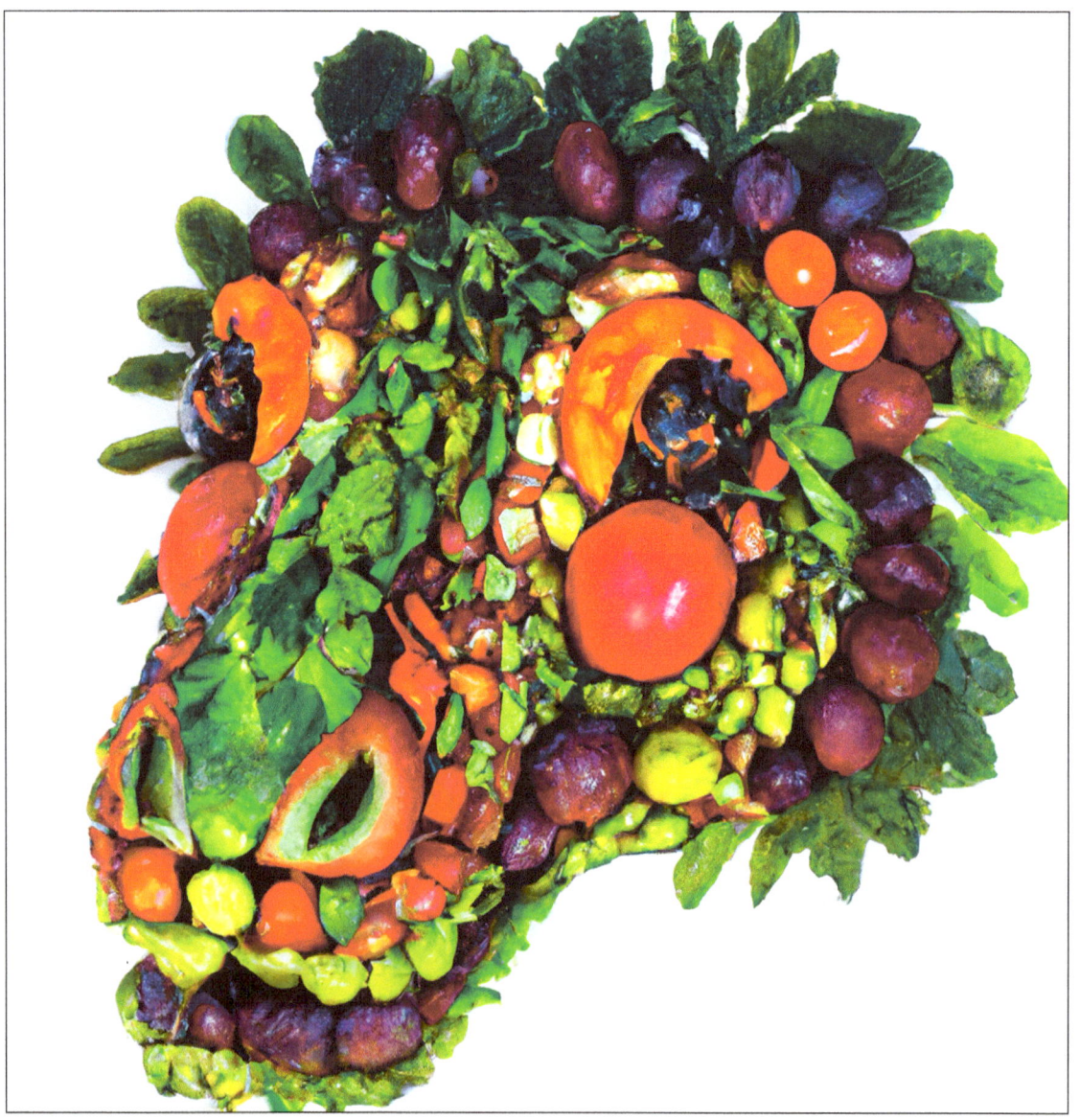

These pages, This crocodile and fish could be made using the same technique and elements as the iguana, dinosaur and fish. We would use shelled pistachios to fill in the crocodile skin. A slice of strawberry could make his nose. The greens for both animals could be any type of lettuce, parsley. The fish tail might be endive. The spikes could be agave or aloe. The fish has slices of citrus in addition to whole small fruits.

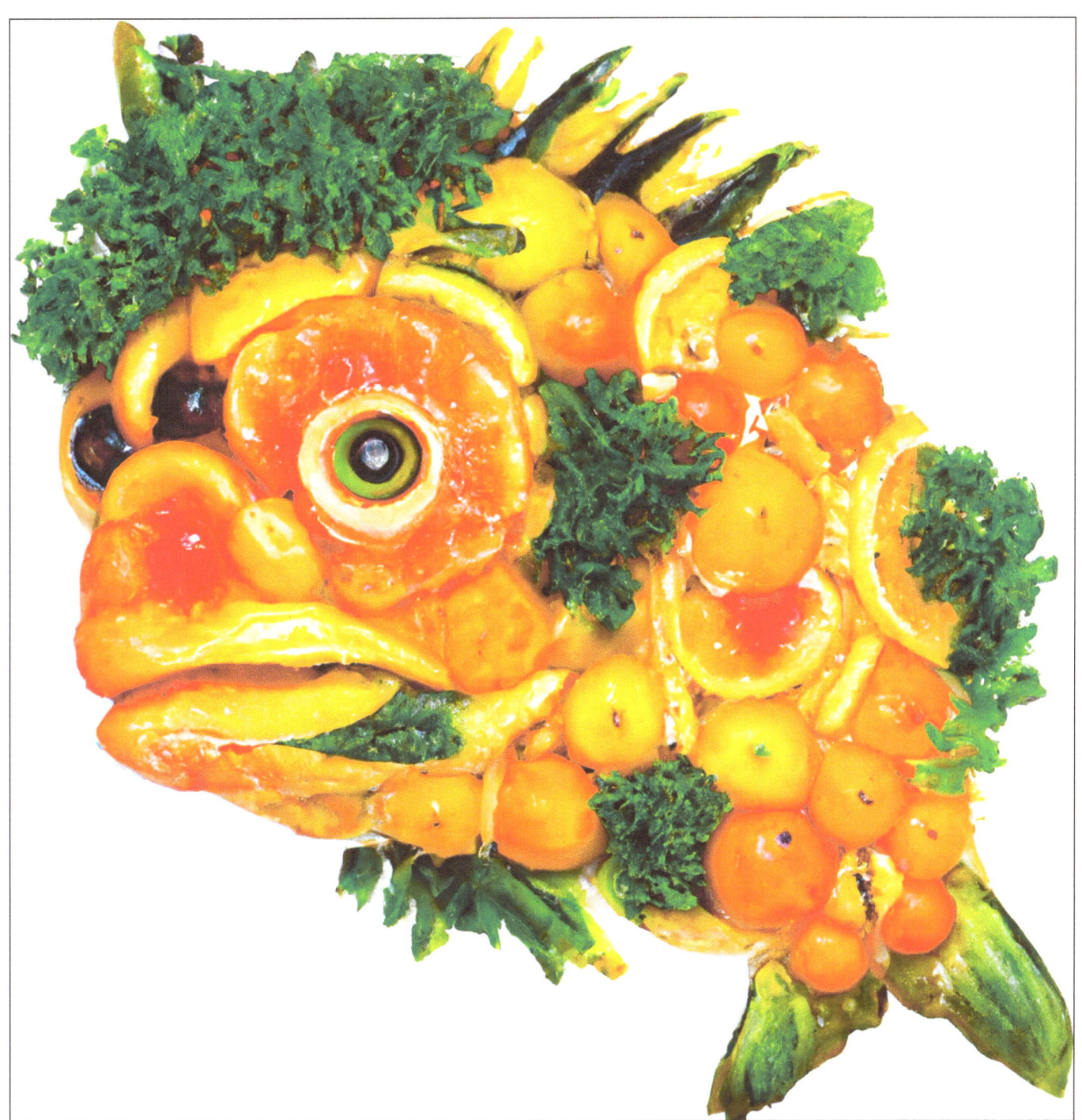

Bird Faces

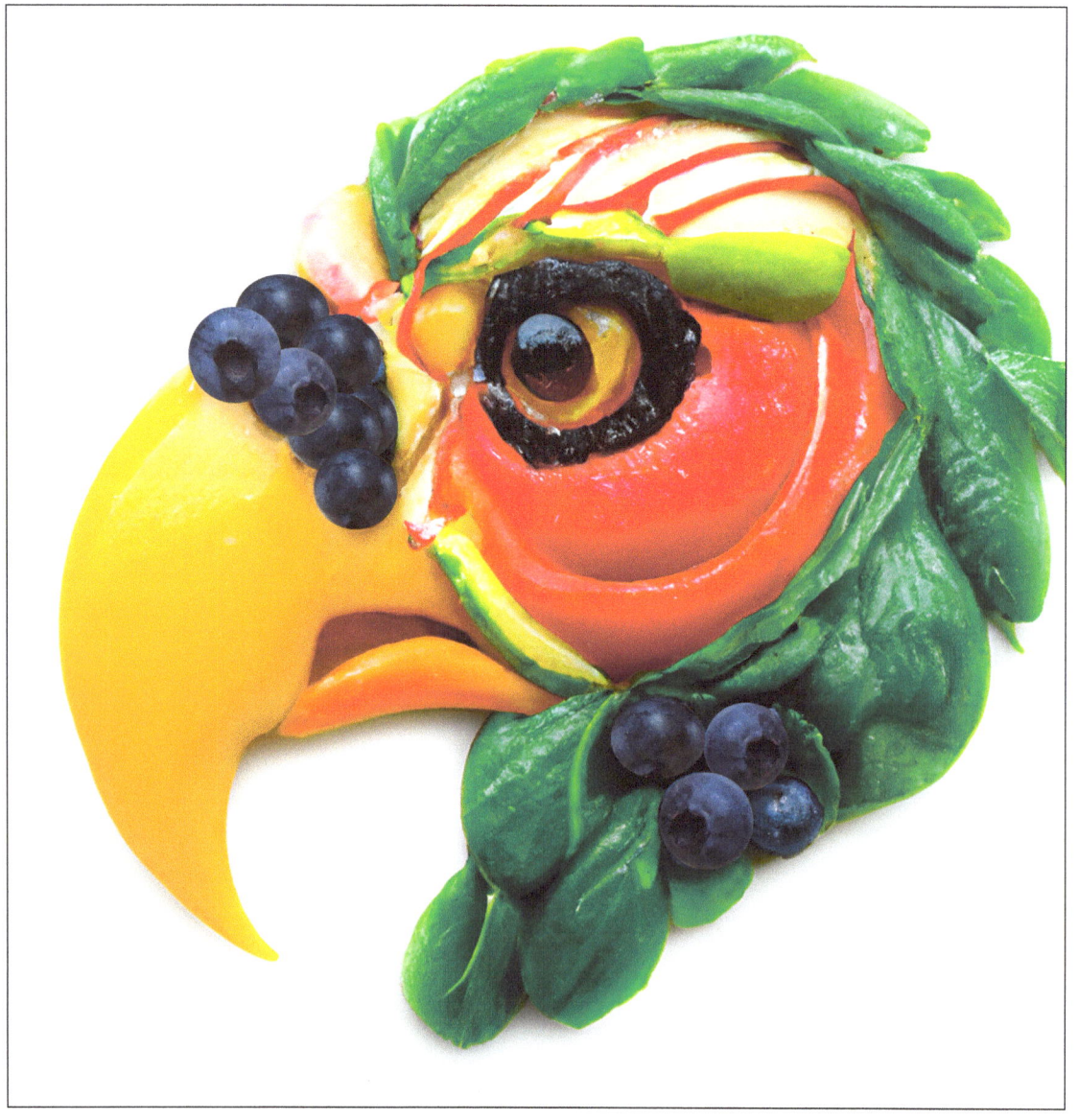

Right, This very stylized humming bird might start with a plum for the head. Small fruits define the shape of the bird's body and lettuce greens could define the feet, tail and wings. His beak can be a slice of purple eggplant or pepper.

Left, The parrot starts with a beak cut from a shiny yellow pepper. His face can be defined by slices of red apple, pepper or other smooth-skinned fruit. For the greens we would use basil leaves. His eye could be a prune with the center removed and a purple grape for an eye. Blueberries finish the bird's head.

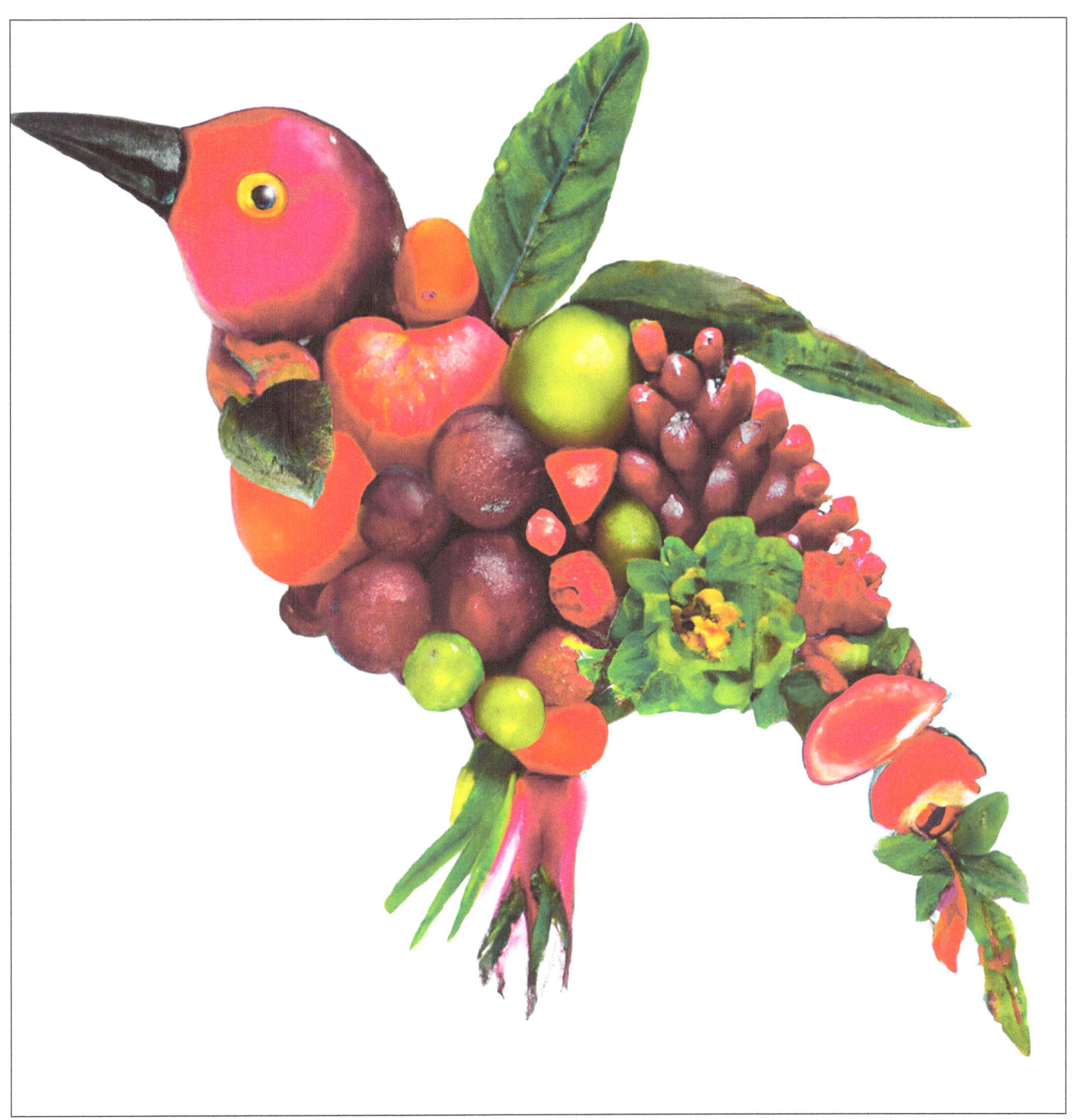

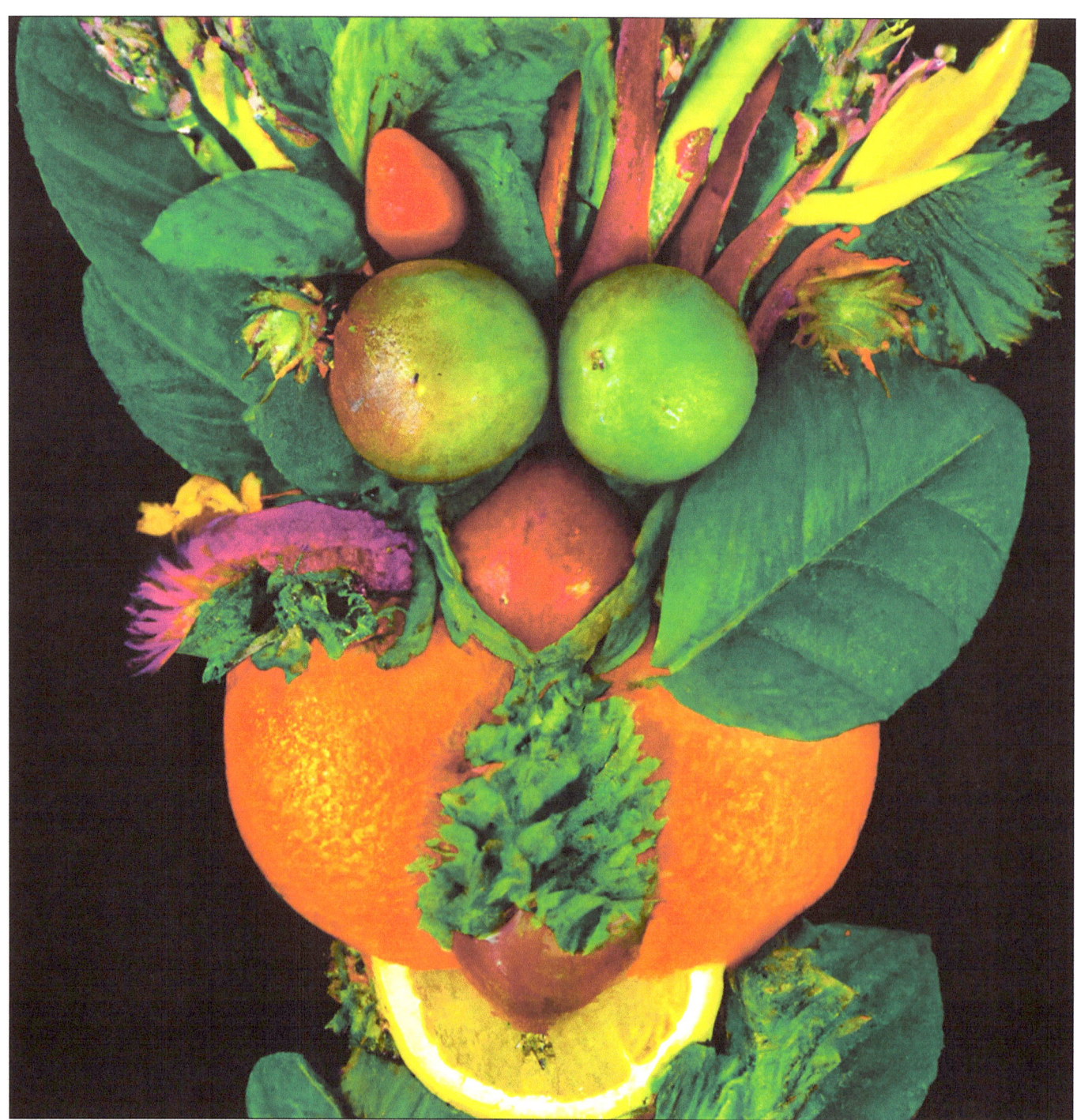

www.ingramcontent.com/pod-product-compliance
Lightning Source LLC
Chambersburg PA
CBHW051829210526
45473CB00005B/1797